How To Love Yourself,
Be Happy With Your Life
And Heal Negative Thoughts

Positive Thinking to Change Your
Mind About Your Problems

Samuel C. A.

Table of Contents

Introduction

Why are habits so difficult to change? Because they are protected by the brain; your brain notices you doing a certain behavior often and seeks to make that behavior as efficient as possible, solidifying it into a habit thanks to muscle memory, conditioning, and repetition. The brain doesn't, however, discern which habits are good and which are bad, especially for the long term.

This book will guide you step-by-step on switching your mindset by using daily rituals to make life more manageable. You have built confidence through your habit building. This book will help you remove the friction on everyday problems by establishing an abundant thinking reward system.

The act of abundant thinking will lead to more self-love; you will have more mental energy to build trust in your ability to maintain this way of thinking. You will see a boost in your self-confidence as you learn to prioritize your mental health more and more each day, and you will walk into a new self-discovery by allowing yourself to become vulnerable to yourself. It is a privileged position because it is easier to achieve personal success when you can thrive in life, not only survive. Abundance thinking may have been challenging but it is worth it. When your race, sexual orientation, and/or gender is seen as fringe or even illegal, your mind can start to accept that the world will never be safe for you. Marginalized people are more likely to experience discrimination from intersectionality and intergenerational trauma. Like many people during the pandemic, being in survival mode is almost always paired with scarcity thinking. This journey into a positive mindset will be challenging for many people, but remember to go easy on yourself and practice at your own pace.

We will focus on accessibility and affordability for all learning exercises and a strong focus on an overall sense of well-being.

Just like in the movie *The Matrix*, Neo, the film's main character, has the choice to continue the self-discovery journey or ignore it and live in ignorance. "Choice is an illusion created between those with power and those without," a quote from the movie.

I'm going to ask you to make a promise—not to me, but to yourself. You can choose to pursue a good life, or do nothing, and remain just however miserable you are. Will you allow yourself to have all the mental power needed to overcome obstacles in your life? Will you allow yourself to finally be happy?

- Yes
- No

Signature: _____

Date: _____

If YES, let's boost your energy with Chapter 1, The Daily Routine.

Chapter 1

The Daily Routine

It's six in the morning, and you force yourself to wake up to get ready for work. You are slowly brushing your teeth and fantasizing about having your coffee in your hands. You finally figure out what to wear after staring at the mirror, trying on different outfits, and eventually landing on one that allows you to fade into the background. Now, you only have enough time to grab a cereal bar quickly. You wish you had more time to make a real breakfast, something that wouldn't make you hungry after an hour of consuming it! You rush out the door and see you just missed your ride to work. Now you're late and starting to ponder if you made the right decision to take this job in the first place?

You finally get to work and apologize for being late. You stare at the clock until you can get away from this desk. Time is moving so slowly. Celebrate that you made it without having a mini breakdown. You reward yourself for making it to the end of the workday with takeout. You are *way* too tired to cook. You make your way back home, open the door, and run to the television to unplug from your mental exhaustion. After eating your take-out, you stay on the couch, relaxing, and lose track of the rest of your night. Before you know it, it's time to go to bed, but not before a dopamine boost from social media. You lose track of time again and fall asleep with your phone. The daily routine continues again and again.

And then it happens—a global pandemic. Everyone is scared to breathe, social distancing starts and people keep farther and farther away from each other. You do as you are told and isolate yourself in your home. Your job has now turned remote, and you wait: Wait for all this to be over.

You are wondering when you can see your family and friends again? You miss your elderly grandparents, but can't see them in person or risk their health. Since your daily routine changed slightly and commuting is no longer a part of your day any-more, you wake up and have time for breakfast. You feel awful saying it, but you needed the break. You were on the verge of burnout. It would help if you could have a vacation before this. How long can this take? A couple of months tops.

About two years into your new remote job, your employer asks you to come back to work physically instead of remotely. You figure you need to reintegrate into society as your social skills have been beaten by the lack of social interaction. You were single before this happened, and now you lost two years on the dating scene. Maybe you're never going to find the one. You can't remember the last time you went on a date. You want to start dating again, and the mask mandate just ended. Perfect timing, but first, you need to get used to commuting to work again.

You go back to work, and within a week, everyone has covid-19, including yourself. After two years, you saw your grandparents, and now you have to wait again. You are scared, you feel like you got hit by a bus, and the physical exhaustion is terrible. You have to take two naps a day to be able to function. You live off takeout. Your social anxiety kicks in, depression sets in, and you feel alone because you *are* alone. You read somewhere that reading transports you to different worlds through storytelling. You give it a try. After reading a book about mental health, you realize your way of thinking is blocking a lot of your blessings. You heal from your symptoms of covid and start to taste and smell regularly again. You continue your search for answers, and you stumble on this book.

Fill your lungs with fresh air, hold that breath for five counts, and then exhale all the air through your mouth. I know it feels like so much has changed in this time, but that doesn't have to be a bad thing.

Rewriting the Routine

Making a safer space involves freedom from discrimination and the ability to express yourself through your vulnerability. This vulnerability is the source of communication with your authentic self, establishing a connection to an inner supportive place. You want to prioritize setting and sticking to a recurring time every day for your safer space. You are isolated from people and distractions, so you do not interrupt the flow state when connecting with your inner supportive place. The best practice in time management for this connection is ideally the morning because it has the most minor distractions.

As you move through chapters, you will slowly be creating a healing music playlist to remind you that you have the power to change the way you think daily. If you don't particularly like or have the same taste in music as I do, I understand—but it couldn't hurt to try, right? Make your own list, if you prefer. No matter how bad the situation may seem, there is always a way to shift your perspective and find a solution by observing different angles.

Let's rewrite this story from a different mindset. What are three good things that happened in this story?

1. You didn't lose your job during the global pandemic. Instead, your life became a bit easier with remote work by living without the stress and expense of commuting to a physical location.
2. You avoided a significant burnout and a breakdown by working beyond your means.
3. You got your taste and smell back after surviving covid!

This exercise is an example of a gratitude journal. At the end of the day, before you go to bed, remember to write down the top three things you are thankful for and write *thank you* after each entry.

Checklist

- Start a daily gratitude journal and write at least one sentence per day. You can journal about anything, and there are no rules except that everything that is written must be something you are grateful for. –Thank you. (See how easy that was?)
- On a separate page, write a journal entry after listening to the song: "Good Job" by Alicia Keys. How did the music make you feel? You'll be doing these for every chapter, so get used to keeping a space separate for your musical interpretation.

Chapter 2

How to Change Your Mind About Your Problems?

Your gut is your second brain! The gastrointestinal system is also vulnerable to experiencing burnout and may even cause mental, physical, and emotional exhaustion.

The gut has a network called the *enteric nervous system (ENS)*; this system is quasi-autonomous. To explain what quasi-autonomous is beyond the simple compounding of two words, let's take the example of a teenager. Teenagers can technically care for themselves but need a form of leadership for guidance. The more mentally healthy that open leadership is, the better overall for the teenager's success. The ENS can function without communicating with the brain; it's a network of neurons in the gastrointestinal walls from your throat to your intestines; they are in charge of keeping everything in order and moving smoothly.

Ayurveda is a practice of South Asian natural medicines and exercises. In the teachings of *Ayurveda*, an unbalanced digestive system is the cause of the majority of the world's diseases and disorders.

Have you ever woken up more exhausted than when you went to bed and had to take a day off for rest because you couldn't do anything that needed mental focus? This feeling of being burnt out mentally is a sign of a lack of homeostasis. *Homeostasis* is a state of being organized, focused, and in harmony with function. A term called gut dysbiosis is when your gut microbiome is out of balance. The gastrointestinal system has trillions of good bacteria and harmful bacteria. Good bacteria protect the *gastrointestinal system (GIS)* from the overpopulation of harmful bacteria, the latter causes inflammation in the gut. This inflamed GIS can become chronic if ignored and can cause burn holes in the GIS and may cause colon cancer. Probiotics (good bacteria) can easily be found in foods like yogurt or buy supplements.

There is a connection between the enteric nervous system and the central nervous system called the gut-brain axis. This gut-brain axis is a direct pathway between the gastrointestinal system and the brain, without obstacles or interruptions. This points to why there is extensive storage of serotonin in the gastrointestinal system. Serotonin is a neurotransmitter that usually gives you the feeling of being happy and an overall feeling of good well-being. This vast storage of serotonin is why gut-directed psychotherapy is on the rise. It shows promise in individual-directed specific symptoms rather than what the general population suffers from.

Studies on serotonin have suggested a correlation between constipation and depression. The study of the gut-brain axis is a growing place of research, and it might explain why we experience emotions in our gut. The gastrointestinal system has more power over the brain than we think.

How does mental health fit into all of this? Your mental health is the current state of your mindset. If you are experiencing many negative thoughts, you are in a negative state of mental health. This negative state of mind is a toxic environment. Others may influence it. For example, unhealthy beauty standards are everywhere in the media and society. This negative external motivation corrupts the mind into a terrible cycle of self-abuse. If you are experiencing an inner dialogue with the majority of positive thoughts, you are in a positive state of mental health. If you have an unhealthy gut microbiome with too many harmful bacteria, the link to depression and anxiety may affect your brain health. Depression and anxiety that starts in the brain can also affect your colon health by inflaming the colon and causing either diarrhea or constipation.

Fake Futures and Fortune-Telling

Depression is reliving the past and wishing for a fake future, and anxiety is fortune thinking and creating fake futures.

What is a fake future? It is a hypothetical situation orchestrated by your anxiety. How many times has your brain made these fake futures? These simulated interactions with people in your head. On a bad day, it could be 120 times per minute!

We do it every day, from the innocent making up a backstory to an exciting stranger as inspiration while on your daily walk to the not-so-innocent mindset of making up hostile confrontations with strangers while on that same daily walk. One walk is good for your mental health, and the other is not.

Awareness is fundamental. You are now aware of fake futures so that you can spot them. It's like your body is fighting COVID with the vaccine, and your body now has an idea of what COVID's appearance is. Now, you can spot a fake future; If you are in the presence of an unreal future, the best thing to do is call it out.

Affirmations are phrases that remind you to stay positive. To keep yourself in a good headspace, repeat affirmations like:

- "I see you, fake future! Goodbye negativity!"
- "I have the power to face reality! I will not run away!"

Getting in your own way translates to negative inner speech stopping you from enjoying your authentic self!

Another form of fake future can come from assimilation. Assimilation is when you interweave into the current domain culture and forget your authenticity. For example, first-generation citizens of a country compared to their immigrant parents.

The other negative aspect of depression, as I mentioned, is reliving the past. As humans, our memory doesn't serve us well. Each time we remember something, we slightly change it. Our memories are closer to a game of telephone than real-life situations.

You and other people influenced can alter the original memory. Your brain can remember things that never happened or things that happened differently from how you remember them. These types of memories are called false memories. Sometimes these false memories can even put an innocent person in jail. When others feed you misinformation about something you have experienced, it can change what you remember. For example, you witness a car accident and are asked if broken glass was at the scene. The act of the person questioning you if there was broken glass is altering the memory if you never paid attention to broken glass in the first place. You are now more likely to answer *yes* just because someone asked.

The other negative aspect of anxiety, on the other hand, is fortune-telling. Fortune-telling is predicting future events or situations. Fortune-telling paired with the fear of anxiety makes for a very uncomfortable time. A widespread form of this fortune-telling anxiety is white coat syndrome; when you feel completely normal at home and when you enter a medical institution, your blood pressure increases.

Your judgment of me is NOT a reflection on my self-worth! Even if I made it up in my mind.

For example, social anxiety is the anxiety of being around people. This anxiety has increased since the global pandemic and the strict restrictions on social distancing due to the COVID-19 outbreak. Social anxiety stems from a lack of trust and a lack of self-esteem because of the fear that people will not accept your authenticity.

"After living in a bubble, it feels awkward blending again," Dr. Monica Vermani writes in *A Deeper Wellness: Conquering Stress, Mood, Anxiety, and Traumas.*

One thing to realize is that change is standard, and so is moving out of your comfort zone. Human beings are innately social creatures, and social anxiety doesn't align with our natural rhythm of being.

High functioning depression, otherwise known as *persistent depressive disorder*, is a form of depression in which individuals can do their daily activities, unlike *major depressive disorder*, which leaves you debilitated and so mentally exhausted that you can not function.

High functioning depression is someone incredibly good at masking their depression from everyone for years. Masking is the act of faking a persona to hide the mental health issues you are dealing with using a fake narrative. People like Anthony Bourdain or Kate Spade are sadly people who lost their battles with high functioning depression. The stigma of calling high functioning depression by the individuals struggling is in us all. It still allows you to engage in society continually, and this stigma has fewer and fewer people with this mental issue to seek help.

Major depressive disorder can leave you in a state much like a person who is grieving over a loved one. Bipolar disorder is experiencing incredibly happy manic episodes paired with very dark depressive episodes, in different variations per individual.

People underestimate your depression because you can function in society, but you are self-critical. You overthink every situation, and that usually burns you out. You might have unhealthy forms of distraction like needing a drink to unwind after a hard day, as you can not shut off the self-critical overthinker. Or maybe you are escaping reality with disassociation by binge-watching a couple of seasons of a television show.

Here are some indicators to look out for in yourself or others for high functioning depression:

- sadness
- crying
- avoiding hobbies
- change in eating habits
- fatigue
- brain fog
- change in sleeping habits
- lack of motivation
- lack of focus
- irritability

Irritability is usually not spoken about, but this indicator is being hyper-annoyed at not being able to be left alone with your depression.

Depression can appear in not-so-apparent characteristics like personalization, should-thinking, and overgeneralizing situations and obstacles that push you out of your comfort zone.

Anxiety can appear in features like mindreading, catastrophizing, and control fallacy situations and barriers that cause you out of your comfort zone.

The comfort zone is a mental space that is routine, familiar, and reliable. It feels like a place of safety, but in reality, it stops you from evolving into your next-level self, the better version of yourself. A safer space is a supportive place where you feel comfortable sharing your vulnerability without judgment or fear of discrimination. A safer space allows you to live in the now as both depression and anxiety rob you of that presence.

There are four essential routines to achieve an excellent healthier overall mindset: *sleep, predictability, preparation,* and *having a support team.*

For the brain-gut axis to function optimally, you must sleep daily. The ideal amount of sleep needed will vary depending on your age and overall health. Ideally, the amount of daily sleep should be part of your daily routine, as a lack of sleep can risk permanently injuring your ENS. Without daily sleep, you might cause a break in the communication of the gut-brain axis. This communication break can cause restrictions on the vagus nerve, which regulates digestion and other involuntary functions.

Sleep It Off

Sleep is the foundation for life, and without prioritizing sleep, no matter how great your food consumption is or how much you exercise per day, you will not be helping your mindset progress to a positive outlook. The truth hurts, but sleep is essential for a positive outlook on life.

Exercise and diet are the main components of a healthier lifestyle pushed in the media. One important aspect they leave out is that exercise and diet are useless without adequate daily sleep. Daily sleep is the foundation of exercise and diet; instead, sleep is step 1, and exercise and diet are step 2. Without daily sleep, you lack focus and attention and are more likely to make errors during awake hours. The brain is just as affected by a lack of sleep as the gut. Studies have found a link between the lack of daily sleep and vaccine effectiveness. Scientists have found that only allowing yourself four hours of sleep a night drops your vaccine effectiveness by 70%. You have the power to make medicines work better for you! Stage 3 and stage 4 of *non-rapid eye movement (NREM)* sleep give the body the right chemicals to incite recovery and reorganization. Sleep is where you heal and indeed continue your longevity in life.

Have you ever wondered why your weight loss goals are not happening year after year? A lack of sleep at a continuous rate will stop weight loss and promote weight gain because you are in survival mode instead of thriving. A lack of sleep while exercising will also increase your chances of injury. The easiest way to get your weight loss goals back on track is to prioritize daily sleep.

Finding out your sleep schedule might be easy if you already know if you are a night owl or morning bird, but if you don't understand, try to wake up without an alarm on an off day. This will allow you to see where you naturally fit on the sleep schedule scale. Scientists have discovered that the 9–5 workday isn't for everyone, and a push for a sustainable work environment is on the agenda of many companies.

Avoid taking caffeine and eating chocolate before sleep, as they can stay in your system for prolonged periods that will affect your ability to have a night of interrupted restful sleep. If you are a morning bird, you want to stop taking caffeine and chocolate at around 12 p.m., noon.

Having a pre-set time of an hour to fall asleep will help you relax; remove all tech like your smartphone and laptop. It will promote a calm space for healing for the mind, body, and soul. Minds craving dopamine can relax by reading a book or listening to calming music to get ready for sleep.

The cure for an anxious mind is writing, a way to physically get the thoughts out of your brain. If you don't like writing, journal using drawing or abstract art to safely allow your external influenced thoughts out of your mind. Sing, do interpretive dance, learn a sport or martial art—something to get those restless thoughts and feelings out of your head.

Keep It Simple, Silly

Predictability is a helpful tool to help automate time-consuming activities in your life. For example, a "capsule wardrobe" is a 20–33 piece clothing and accessories collection. Every item can be worn together, and there is a consistent style and color palette. The form of predictability will save you money, space, and time for your fashion expression. It is a great way to pack a vacation or business trip.

Example of a mini capsule wardrobe:

1. black t-shirt
2. white t-shirt
3. gray t-shirt
4. black jeans
5. dark blue jeans
6. light blue jeans
7. one black pair of shoes
8. one white pair of shoes
9. one black carrier bag
10. one black backpack

Burnout culture is part of the capitalistic world we live in, where consumerism is at the forefront of society. The more we consume this culture, the more "stuff" we have to distract us from our own health and well-being.

Let's explore the minimalist lifestyle—we have already reviewed the minimalistic and eco-friendly way of fashion expression called the capsule wardrobe. On average, you will only use 10% of your closet. Why store clothing and accessories that you will never wear? Hoarding 90% of your closet for a fake future that doesn't exist doesn't make sense. The minimalist lifestyle is only to keep items essential to your way of life. Minimalism is a simplified way of living without the extra baggage weighing you down.

The global pandemic has stressed the need to take inventory of your essentials. Name ten essentials of your current life:

1. _____

2. _____

3. _____

4. _____

5. _____

6. _____

7. _____

8. _____

9. _____

10. _____

How many of the essentials above are classed as sentimental? A sentimental essential consistently gives you a nostalgic feeling of remembering a person or an event. Sentimental items can also sometimes trigger memories of that person or event.

Minimalism focuses you on asking the question:

How might your life be better with less?

This question allows you to organize your life to have more time to prioritize your relationships, hobbies, financial success, and health. It gives you a more straightforward version of what you want to get out of life.

The act of minimalism will lower your overall waste and debt. You start to consume less so you can live more. Minimalism is about relearning to love people over obsessive consumerism of unessential things.

The act of predictability will allow for a more sustainable lifestyle.

Hobbies are another example of predictability in action. Hobbies decrease stress by removing capitalism, removing the need to make money off an activity. You must enjoy the hobby enough to sustain doing it for no financial gain. The act of remembering the hobby should evoke an emotion of joy. Hobbies are done strictly for fun. For example, you play video games for fun and are not a professional gamer.

List three activities you do for fun:

1. _____
2. _____
3. _____

Some tips to decrease your daily stress with predictability include having an organized schedule, going for daily walks, and scheduling time alone.

Preparation is another essential routine for triggers and other issues that happen in daily life. Sound therapy is healing through the use of sound, like music. Music is used as a reminder or helps take you on a musical journey from anxious to calm. Music is a safer space because of the range of emotions usually displayed in vocals and beats. A good practice is to have a daily playlist that reminds you and your inner child that you are safe, seen, and heard. This daily playlist will give you the power to not be influenced by external forces.

Affirmations and Meditations

Affirmations can be found in songs, or you can make up your own personal affirmations, depending on your current situation.

"I'm okay right now."

"I am powerful."

"I love myself."

These affirmations are meant to be simple, so recall is easier. Affirmations are excellent for snapping the brain out of control and allowing your complete conscious control.

With the majority of the population being mentally exhausted, meditation is a freeway for self-reflection, removing anxiety, and a boost of energy to your gut health.

1. Find a comfortable position. For example, sit cross-legged with your back resting on the wall or sitting in a chair.
2. Close your eyes and focus on your breath. Inhale and Exhale.
3. Use the 4-4-4 technique: Inhale for four counts, hold for four counts, exhale for four counts.
4. Witness your thoughts get your attention. Allow them one sentence to explain themselves, respond with

"thank you for your concern," and then show them the exit.

5. Become the observer; witness the way your thoughts get your brain's attention, and how you start to distance yourself from the thoughts.
6. Practice for one minute a day

Make your day more predictable with daily meditation; there are many different types to try, be they guided or alone.

Three-Minute Thoughts

- one minute meditation
- one minute journal
- one minute read

There are no rules except for the minimum time of one minute for each item. One minute for observation; one minute for anxiousness cure; one minute for inspiration. This mental health exercise will help you relax and calm down in stressful situations.

Meditation can come in many forms, including dancing, singing, painting, and even playing instruments. If you have watched the animated movie *Soul,* the flow feeling is shown as magical energy, but it is truly that! You lose track of time and even forget hunger when entering into a flow state of mind. Meditation allows your soul to take charge and your mind to come much-needed rest.

Some tips to decrease your daily stress with preparation include prepping for meals, having an emergency protocol for triggers, and organizing chores.

Who You Gonna Call?

A support system is a living, breathing, safer space in human form. A support group usually consists of four to five people who love you unconditionally. Your support system should have genuine people with an interest in your well-being.

As humans are social creatures, the pandemic has really strained support groups. Many people worldwide have experienced loss in their support group, either if a member has passed or exited the group from lack of a social network. Use technology to help support your support system for regular check-ins.

To create a strong support team, make a routine for a regular check-in.

- text at least once a week
- call bi-weekly
- in-person meet every month

Suppose you have noticed a member taking advantage of the support group. In that case, you must voice your concerns as one person's negativity can spread to others and eradicate the support system.

This support is often neglected or abused by toxic people or a toxic environment. If you feel like you are being taken advantage of in a support system you belong to, try to voice your concerns. Being part of someone else's support system is still a place of non-judgment and free of discrimination for all members involved. If you are met with emotional abuse, please leave the support group as it is not a safe space for you.

If you have trust issues from a toxic support system, it will take you a little longer to become vulnerable to non-toxic people again, as being vulnerable is something the mind tries to avoid because it's a practice that lives in the present moment rather than the past or future. The mind's power over your consciousness is the most powerful in these times.

Who would you call if you were in the hospital badly injured, or who would you call if you just won the lottery? A valuable person in your ideal support system would get both of these calls. No matter the situation, you want them involved.

Name your support system:

1. _____

2. _____

3. _____

4. _____

5. _____

If you can't find enough people for your support team, don't worry, the majority of the world's population feels the same. This list is a case of quality over quantity. It might have a partial support system list, or you need to start over. With patience and dedication, you will find your tribe one day! A group of five individuals who love you unconditionally and encourage you to be your authentic self every day.

When reorganizing your support system, one thing to watch out for is trauma bonding. Trauma bonding is an unhealthy attachment to a toxic relationship, and it can range from parent to child, abuser to the victim, and friend to friend. The abuse can be either emotional or physical, or both. If you suspect a trauma bond in your current support group, it needs to be removed slowly and carefully, as the usual end is explosive.

Some tips to decrease your daily stress with a support system include scheduling monthly physical outings, weekly phone calls, and daily texts to your support system.

Making friends with social anxiety is tricky as rejection sensitivity can stop you from trying anything with other people. Start slowly. Pick one person in the community you live in and engage in conversation. Please keep it simple about yourself, then ask open-ended questions to the person you have chosen. The person can not answer the open-ended question with a simple yes or no. For example, "My name is John, and what's yours?" They say their name, and you reply, "Nice to meet you." This first interaction is where you gauge the conversation. Have you been invited with non-verbal cues to continue or end the conversation? The conversation might continue with you saying, "I see you around sometimes, and I want to tell you that your jacket is amazing. Thank you for the inspiration." and that might be the end of it; each day gives the same amount of effort. Slowly watch your friendship blossom.

There is a way to stop being manipulated by toxic people, practicing the art of *high-value self-worth (HV)*. Demonstrating high-value self-worth is the ability to showcase your worth and put up boundaries when your worth is undervalued. An example of HV is having a toxic friend spread rumors about you, and you end the friendship. Showing lower self-worth means allowing others to disrespect and undervalue you. An example of low self-worth is if a toxic friend continuously borrows money from you and spreads rumors about you simultaneously.

How to spot a toxic friend:

- They are emotionally defensive over their actions
- They have crossed your boundaries multiple times.
- They have a behavioral pattern of drama.
- They humiliate you in public at your expense.
- They are emotionally abusive.
- They compete with you for attention.
- They sabotage your happiness.

The bare minimum is being able to trust your physical, mental, emotional, and spiritual safety. The bare minimum is receiving unconditional love and your authenticity being respected and honored. This bare minimum is the foundation of all healthy relationships. It is all about quality over quantity with healthy relationships that allow you to evolve as change is the only consistent in this world.

How to spot a good friend:

- They are always laughing with you.
- They prioritize spending time with you.
- They are supportive in the bad moments in your life.
- They encourage you to follow your passions.
- They practice honesty with kindness.
- They accept your authenticity.

A lot of support groups have disappeared because of the pandemic fallout. *Pandemic fallout* is a term for friendship that didn't last during the global pandemic. If you start this journey without a support group, you will know what you are looking for in a friend by the end of this chapter. When you apply for a job, the employer knows who they need on their team; the same goes for making friendships.

So, how do we figure out what we are looking for in a friendship?

Love Languages

Love languages are different ways you express how you would like to receive and give intimacy and affection.

The different types of love languages are:

- words of affirmation
- quality time
- receiving gifts
- acts of service
- physical touch

Please keep in mind that you can have more than one love language, and you can have a difference depending on if you are the giver or receiver of the love in question.

Words of affirmation: These are words of encouragement. Motivational and inspirational words or phrases like "You got this" or "I'm so happy for you." These types of affirmations work just like affirmations you say to yourself. Still, because it comes from someone who shows you unconditional love and respects your authenticity, it is also paired with validation of the particular affirmation. You believe the support team member, as sometimes belief in your own words is difficult depending on the situation at hand.

Quality time: This reflects how much effort a support member gives you through time. You can practice quality time with either a one-on-one designated time or an in a group setting, and the central aspect is that no one is distracted or interrupting the quality time. Quality time is a place of vulnerability. A friend that comes over every Saturday for brunch is a great example; the friend has carved out time to share with you.

Receiving gifts: This love language is pretty straightforward. Gift giving is a standard form of appreciation in current society, from birthdays to personal achievements. It is sometimes challenging to know if you fully have this love language or if society is thinking for you. The best practice is to journal your reaction after receiving or giving gifts. Receiving gifts should give you a sense of validation while giving gifts should give you a sense of altruism.

Acts of service: How do you feel when someone does a task you were supposed to do? This love language makes someone's life a little easier, taking away some stress from the recipient's life. Imagine you are having an extremely stressful day at work. You finally get to lunch break, and your co-worker offers to buy you lunch and take you out for drinks after work. This love language is exclusive to altruism, which is the act of kindness without needing them in return.

Physical touch: Touch is something many people need, and we have seen how the lack of it can negatively affect our mental health through the global pandemic. Human beings are innately social creatures. Physical touch can translate from a handshake to a hug to sexual intimacy. It all depends on what you need or what you are willing to offer. This love language is now becoming exclusively about vulnerability as the global pandemic has caused all of humanity to be more conscious about interacting physically with someone other than yourself.

What are your love languages, and what love languages do you prefer to give? This answer will depend on the type of love you receive or give to others.

Giving:

- _____
- _____
- _____

Receiving:

- ----------------------------------
- ----------------------------------
- ----------------------------------

There are two forms of love in support systems: conditional love and unconditional love.

Conditional love: This form of toxic abuse is only given under certain circumstances. It is framed almost like a prize or privilege to acquire. Conditional love tolerates the recipient and is often used as a form of control.

Unconditional love: This form of respect is given under all circumstances. There are no conditions to be met to attain this form of love. Unconditional love accepts the recipient's authenticity and is often proud of the recipient.

A chosen family is the family you choose to have, and a given family is your family members. How can someone not related to you love you more unconditionally than your own blood family? Why does your given family take you for granted and offer more conditional love than unconditional love? Authenticity is accepted with novelty rather than with routine. The more familiar the social interaction without respect, the more likely conditional love outweighs the safety of vulnerability. A safer space does not have conditional love present.

A child who goes through this lack of unconditional love and neglect will become hyper-independent and prone to burnout.

The lack of guidance on what unconditional love looks or feels like will cause you to romanticize what it may be like to depend on someone because of how mentally exhausted you are doing it all alone. That romanticism of dependence will also create a romance around creating fake futures of less mental exhaustion. Humans are social beings, and we need social connections to survive.

Disassociation and lack of unconditional love as a child—imagine being neglected by the people that are supposed to love you unconditionally and being able to admit that they are most likely never to show the unconditional love you so deeply desire. It is okay to have family members that are acquaintances. You are allowed not to like the people you love unconditionally; that's okay. It is also okay not to put as much effort into an acquaintance relationship as a friendship.

Make a list of all the names of your friends and family members and circle either acquaintance (A) or friend (F) based on how close your relationship is. Who would you call if you were dying if you needed an emergency contact?

- _____(A/F)
- _____(A/F)
- _____(A/F)
- _____(A/F)
- _____(A/F)
- _____(A/F)
- _____(A/F)

- _____(A/F)
- Emergency Contact: _____

Ask yourself the question, are you a stranger to yourself?

What is the difference between being alone and being lonely? Being alone is a safer space for you without distraction or interruption. Being lonely lacks connection with other human beings and a lack of connection with yourself.

The benefits of prioritizing alone time include:

1. Time to reflect on your interests and find yourself a hobby.
2. Become more independent.
3. Journal with your inner child, and become your own best friend.
4. Your authenticity is always respected and accepted.
5. Practice gratitude and appreciation for one's self.

A great example of clarity from alone time is the ability to know what you want to do for monetary gain. Find out your expertise, find the market for your expertise, and do the hard work to reach your financial goal. Another great example is traveling on your own without companionship, which allows you to explore your strengths and weaknesses on your own.

An extreme way to shock this realization is through a silent meditation retreat. These are offered worldwide, food and lodging are included, and you usually pay what you can. They start with 12 days of silence, and afterward, you can do shorter participation. Your mind will fight you so hard at the beginning that you will want to run home to check if everything is okay because you have no access to any of your tech or given writing or reading. Meditation is the art of doing nothing and being emotionally self-sufficient to remain doing nothing.

The disadvantages of experiencing loneliness:

1. You are in constant survival mode.
2. You are 29% more likely to have heart disease.
3. You are 32% more likely to have a stroke.
4. You are twice as likely to get dementia.

Loneliness is a bigger killer than obesity, and everyone experiences being lonely in their life. Children and the elderly are the most at risk of loneliness.

Ask yourself these questions:

- What are your top five accomplishments in your life?
- What is your favorite non-physical trait about yourself?
- What are you overthinking?
- How would you describe your ideal safer space?

Reflect and journal about the uncomfortable feeling you got when answering these questions.

When you start to notice all the complexities you hold, it becomes easier not to judge others; you have no idea what others are struggling with or without. Good communication practice is to listen without the intent to reply and restrict your technology time to prioritize time to reflect.

Your brain is a muscle that needs to be exercised by workouts, just like your physical body. This muscle has finally gotten a break to rest and avoid burnout. You can now reflect on your own life rather than making judgments on others, creating fake futures, and remembering false memories.

Remember to be patient with your results.

Your gut health is directly linked to your mindset with the gut-brain axis, meaning your gut health can affect your mental state. Bad gut health may result in a negative attitude and increase the duration of mental health issues. Put the control in your hands and focus on how you experience a bowel movement; ask, is it painful? Increase vegetables and fruit consumption and decrease the "standard American diet" (cheeseburgers, greasy pizza, fast food, etc.) eaten per day.

Predictability and preparation will help you organize the chaos in your life. You will be amazed at all the free time you will possess after prepping your life for things to move more smoothly in life. You allow yourself to become the editor of your life story.

The members of your support team are the cheerleaders of your life journey, and making sure your support system is free of toxic friendships and conditional love is crucial to the success of the positive mindset. Your support should be a breathing, living, safer space for you to be vulnerable without discrimination. Prioritizing unconditional love to your support team allows you to return the feeling of access to a safer space and strengthen the team as a whole. Lastly, prioritize your alone time, as this is where you get all your answers about what you need from this healing journey.

Checklist

- Continue your daily gratitude journal.
- Add a journal entry about listening to the song: "Relax, Take It Easy" by Mika. How did the music make you feel?
- Create your own personal affirmation, you will be repeating this mantra at a minimum one time a day.
- Participate in a one-minute meditation every day for one month.
- Remove one unessential item from your life for one month.
- Prioritize your gut health by observing how you feel after a bowel movement.
- What are your love languages?

Chapter 3

How Does This Impact You?

Positive psychology is the study of all these principles combined. How are we able to conquer our inner demons, and how do we even get these demons in the first place?

Grief and rejection both have a way of throwing the positive mindset out the window. You completely forget your emergency protocol, and you are left with no energy, only sadness. Grief and rejection show you that you are missing out on opportunities, but in honesty, you were never meant for those opportunities. Grief is a reflection of the past, while rejection reflects a fake future.

Let's define a trigger; a trigger is a reaction to an emotional catalyst. You need to feel your safety is at risk for a trigger to occur. Two things to keep in mind are: the intersectionality of your definition of the word "safe," and that the memory of the emotional catalyst is enough to start a trigger. A trigger warning is an alert to possibly being triggered; it may be wise to hold off reading the following to protect your mental health. You can abbreviate some words because sometimes the words themselves can alert the subconscious mind.

Who Is the Inner Child?

The inner child is one's authentic self—you, before the age of six or seven, including all those observations you made on life before adequately comprehending what was going on. Think back to your earliest memory; most people can only go back to the earliest memory to age six. What can you remember from your earliest memory? How does it make you feel? Write down your response. This response will help you understand your inner child more profoundly; you will reveal the moment you started to comprehend what was happening in your life.

Any form of abuse at a young age, including emotional, spiritual, mental, and physical, can destroy your positive mindset if you are tricked into believing you are not worthy of the abuser's unconditional love and therefore are not worthy of even your self-love.

The thoughts in your mind can manifest more often the more energy is given to them. For example, you are in the market to buy a mini cooper car, and now all you can see are mini cooper cars everywhere. If you put all your energy into the abusive negative thoughts, they will become your reality.

What is manifestation? *Manifestation* is a belief in one's own personal power to achieve spiritual growth; the proof of an abstract idea—what the heck is that? A manifestation is a "believing it before you see it" experience. The English language does no justice. Let's think about karma; how does karma work? Good deeds make good karma, and evil deeds make bad karma. So, what defines the words good and evil? Are the terms subjective or objective? Karma is a belief in one's personal view on public morals.

Harmful inner speech is not your thoughts, and it's a reminder of the toxic communication of others. It's you catastrophizing the idea of "What will people say?" Disconnect yourself from that dialogue. You are the authority figure for your mind, not anyone else.

What is spiritual growth? Spiritual growth is overcoming subconscious trauma and rebuilding inner child communication.

Let's change some words for clarity:

Manifestation = *Prayer* = A wish you don't ever give up on.

Inner child = *Authenticity* = Your true self, before responsibilities.

Spiritual growth = *Emotional maturity* = Your soul has a say in your life.

Has the altering of these words changed your perspective on them?

Your perspective on your mindset will usually lean towards negative (most commonly) or positive. You are in charge of your mindset, not these false memories and fake futures.

Connect with your inner child with a journal exercise called inner child journaling. Try this on an off day or one where you feel safe and strong, as it might become emotional.

1. Say hello to your inner child through your words on the page.
2. Find out if pronouns are the same as your current ones.
3. Ask a question about your childhood for inspiration.
4. Then ask about a trigger. You may start to cry here as the vulnerability will lower your guarded internal walls.
5. Remember to come from a place of non-judgment, as this is a child, after all.

It is good to take a nap after your initial meeting, as many completely ignore their inner child. Inner child journaling might be a very foreign experience to you. Make a plan to celebrate the connection you have reestablished, and meditation is critical after this experience to relax the mind from shock.

Manifestation and spiritual growth go hand and hand. The manifestations are the goals you create for your spiritual leveling up. This connection will allow you to disconnect from false memories and fake futures, accurately representing your true authentic self.

The choice is yours. Are you going to stay on auto-pilot or learn how to fly this mindset?

Checklist

- Continue your daily gratitude journal and write at least one sentence per day.
- On a separate page, write your music journal entry after listening to the song: "Acouscous" by Emawk. How did the music make you feel?

- Identify your personal triggers.
- Create a manifestation.
- What is your preparation plan for your triggers?
- Continue your meditation and introduce the thought of perspective change.
- Continue your minimalistic cleanse.

Chapter 4

How to Fix the Problem

Building a safer space will be part of your healing journey and transitioning from scarcity thinking to abundance thinking. A safer space is supportive of your vulnerability; this vulnerability is allowed to express authenticity and is met with unconditional self-love. A safer space is also a place of no discrimination or judgment of yourself.

Let's start by increasing your water intake.

Drink Up

Why is water so essential for your overall well-being?

60% of your body is water, and if you are thirsty, you're already dehydrated. When dehydrated, your skin is more vulnerable to infection through dryness; this vulnerability is why people with skin disorders like eczema have to be extra careful with their dry skin, as they may experience splits, cuts, and open wounds from their skin disorders. The cartilage in between your joints is made up of around 80% of water, and when the cartilage is dehydrated, its ability to absorb shock decreases. The blood that delivers oxygen all over your body is 90% water, and dehydration can even affect your blood clotting abilities. Sweat, which is 99% water, helps you cool down when it is too hot for your body. Dehydration can also lead to kidney stones, wrinkles, and restrictions in your airways. The moral of the story is, please drink water daily.

How much water should you be drinking?

An easy way to remember how much water to drink daily is your weight in pounds to the same number in ounces of water. For example, If you weigh 120 pounds, you would drink 120 ounces, which is 3.5 liters of water (nearly a gallon). This amount of water daily might seem like a lot at first but imagine how dehydrated you are if you feel this way. Start slowly with one liter of water a day and eliminate carbonated drinks, juices, and alcohol. Herbal teas can also replace coffee. The journey of increasing your daily water intake is at your own pace.

Let us go through a daily routine step-by-step with a positive mindset; that is the main priority (keep in mind that this is the ideal version of someone's daily routine and that your daily routine may look similar or completely different):

- Wake up after 7–9 hours of restful, uninterrupted sleep.
- Start a high-frequency playlist.
- Drink a glass of water.
- Wait thirty minutes until breakfast.
- Use the washroom.

- Yoga healthy gut warmup and full-body 15-minute workout.
- Have a shower.
- Start the workday meditation.
- Start the workday.
- Drink a glass of water.
- Low-glycemic breakfast with a fruit smoothie.
- Wear a pre-selected outfit for the day.
- Start work as a remote worker.
- Drink a glass of water.
- Leave the home office every two hours for a ten-minute walk.
- Meal prep lunch, drink a glass of water.
- Use the washroom.
- One hour lunch away from home office.
- Leave the home office every two hours for a ten-minute walk.
- End of the work day.
- Drink a glass of water.
- Start a low-frequency playlist.
- Wear a pre-selected outfit for the night.
- Enjoy an end of workday meditation.
- Journal.
- Read.
- Me time; watch your shows.
- Have a low-glycemic dinner with a hot liquid drink of choice.
- Enjoy hobbies.

- Do your one-hour pre-sleep routine, including an entry in your gratitude journal.
- When you are ready, the lights are off, and with the help of blackout curtains, an eye mask, and earplugs—you fall into a beautiful seven to nine hour sleep.

Write down all the similarities you see in your current daily routine compared to the positive mindset example. Then write down all the differences you see in your everyday daily routine compared to the positive mindset example.

Similarities:

- _____
- _____
- _____
- _____
- _____

Differences:

- _____
- _____
- _____
- _____
- _____

Are there any aspects of this positive mindset example **you can implement today**?

- ----------------------

- ----------------------

- ----------------------

Go With the Flow

Imagine you are an artist and have a major project coming up. You do significant projects all the time, and you have gotten a knack for easily or immediately getting into the zone for your projects. You have a morning, mid-day, and evening routine to keep you at a high frequency for efficiency. You have stringent deadlines, and you don't have any time to waste.

Artists and athletes are known for entering "the flow" or "the zone" quickly and sometimes on command, but how can regular people do the same? Flow is a deep concentration on something. This type of concentration has no sense of time, and even your feeling of hunger disappears.

- *Morning routine*: You wake up rested. You allow yourself to detach from society through meditation or with assistance like a cup of warm tea. Then walk right into your flow routine. It consists of all five senses: sight, sound, smell, taste, and touch. You start with the taste of your breakfast. Then you enter the sense of smell with the incense stick. You turn on your high-energy playlist and create sound therapy. Touch enters your flow routine with a full-body workout followed by a shower. Ending the flow routine with a nature walk is a present for the eyes and inspiration for your soul. Then check your schedule.

- *Mid-day routine*: Step away from your workday and have a low-glycemic lunch while watching a comedy to re-charge through laughter. You are at one liter of water in your daily water intake.
- *Evening routine:* You need to come down from the flow state when completing your workday. Your de-flow practice starts with a low-energy playlist consisting of soothing soul music. You make a change in scent from sandalwood to lavender. You slow yourself down with a meditation near your makeshift pond in the garden, watching ripples in the water and listening to the birds. You have dinner with friends tonight, you haven't seen some of them in years, and you are eager for hugs and conversations.

There are four ways to trigger or start flow by increasing dopamine in the brain:

1. novelty
2. unpredictability
3. complexity
4. awe

What is novelty? Novelty is the experience of something new and exciting.

What do we mean by unpredictability? It would help if you released the control you want over the project you want the flow for, and if you're mentally secure enough to be unsure about the path of progress yet stay curious about the outcome.

Why is complexity necessary? To enter the flow, you need the challenge to be slightly more complex than your skill, and this can only happen if you are comfortable with being uncomfortable. The comfort zone is a mental space that is routine, familiar, and reliable. It feels like a place of safety, but in reality, it stops you from evolving into your next-level self, the better version of yourself. Thinking outside the box for layered and challenging problem solving will enlighten a dopamine response.

Awe is the feeling of understanding you are so small compared to the vases of the universe. Let that sink in. You are a speck compared to how huge the universe is. The realization that your problems don't exist in comparison to global issues should help keep your perspective focused on what's important.

This Too Shall Pass

Intrinsic motivators are behaviors that are awakened by a natural inner joy. These motivators establish flow by being linked to each other:

1. curiosity (gives focus)
2. focus (brings purpose)
3. purpose
4. autonomy to pursue (faith in self)
5. mastery

How does curiosity give you focus? Have you ever tried to get the attention of someone while they were interested in something? For example, your child is watching their favorite tv show, and you are trying to feed them. When we are curious we will escape time and start to lose focus on everything except for our hyperfocus.

Why is focus only second in the order of intrinsic motivators when the flow is deep concentration? Deep focus is useless without a purpose as dopamine increases are linked to anything that gives us any sense of pleasure. For example, social media is filled with dopamine hits to your brain, which provides you with that intense focus. Still, it is hard to break away from the dopamine hits because they are simply addictive without purpose.

How does purpose give you autonomy to pursue? Autonomy to pursue, otherwise known as intrinsic motivation, needs a goal to grow. The purpose is that goal; in other words, this is the moment when intrinsic motivation is activated. Your purpose is that magic that comes naturally to you and activates this intrinsic motivation. This activation means once you get to this stage, you will stop adding to the goal and let the goal grow on its own now—for example, farming. Autonomy to pursue is the blind faith you have for your purpose.

Why is autonomy to pursue important to flow? Having faith in your ability to achieve success is the key to a flow state by removing the harmful inner speech. That negative inner voice once convinced you not to try in fear of what others may think of you. That inner voice doesn't exist anymore because you have gained your authority back. You are the only authority figure for your mindset.

Mastery is becoming an expert in something you are interested in with continuous learning in the subject. Becoming a master at something allows you to explore innovation by having the ability to see angles that non-masters can not see. This innovation can lead you to become a pioneer in the industry you have mastery.

Flow (or being "in the zone") is the result of wanting to fix the mindset on your problems, but how do you get there?

Flow is actually the end result; there are three steps before and one step after flow. The five steps to a positive mindset for daily problem solving are:

1. motivation
2. learning and unlearning
3. creativity
4. flow
5. mastery

These steps to flow and how to maintain flow must happen in this order.

Keep 'em Motivated

Motivation is the first level of an inner state of flow. Motivation is a response to something that interests you and is rewarded with dopamine. Dopamine is a neurotransmitter that lets you experience pleasure: that pleasure could be anything from eating tasty food to an orgasm.

We have four different types of motivation:

1. extrinsic motivation
2. intrinsic motivation
3. introjected motivation
4. identified motivation

Extrinsic motivation: This motivation comes from an external force like teachers, employers, or society. External forces motivate you to complete a goal or task because it aligns with your need or wants for certain things. For example, money is an extrinsic motivator for an employer to get you to perform specific tasks for their company.

Intrinsic motivation: This motivation comes from an internal force like pride, authenticity, or curiosity. You are motivating yourself to succeed at a chosen goal or task because of the alignment with your inner desires or essentials. For example, you complete a course in a subject that interests you and gain knowledge in the field of interest.

Introjected motivation: This intrinsic motivation is about observing a goal or task and becoming frustrated with yourself with the lack of progress towards that goal or mission. Then you internally force yourself to prioritize the intent to increase the likelihood of success. For example, you want to lose weight, and for years you have been saying "I will go to the gym three times a week," but you never do. And then, one day, it just clicks, and you start your journey of going to the gym regularly.

You love going to the gym now, and you wonder why you didn't do this earlier.

Identified motivation: This intrinsic motivation is about observing your goal or task and spotting the restrictions and obstacles you have to achieve success. You determine what needs to be done to complete the job or plan. When you can identify the problem, then you can formulate a solution. For example, you need to complete the LSAT exam to become accepted to law school, but afterward, you still need to apply or start a law firm to practice law.

The particular motivation we will focus on is intrinsic, as we are working on creating positive inner speech about our daily problems. For example, low glucose levels (sugar) in your body will trigger the hormone called ghrelin. This hormone makes you feel hungry and reminds you to eat food to increase glucose levels in your body. If you ignore the innate motivation of hunger, your body will enter a stage of food obsession and a state similar to major depressive disorder. You will not want to talk to anyone, have extreme fatigue, and have the inability to focus.

Intrinsic motivation as a whole is the ability to motivate yourself. How can you increase your intrinsic motivation for a particular task or goal?

1. Brainstorm reasons why you find it interesting.
2. Research the particular task or goal for positive connections.
3. Set a plan of action.
4. Plan a celebration after completion.

This list will allow you to see the task or goal as a positive addition to your overall life. This positivity will fuel your positive mindset to continue pursuing the completion of this mission.

Consider: **What is something you have been putting off lately?**

Learning and unlearning is the second level. This level in your inner flow creation story will focus on your curiosity about your routine. You have probably heard of the line "Curiosity killed the cat," but we have only been taught half the quote.

Curiosity Killed the Cat, but Satisfaction Brought It Back

Let's break down what this all means. What is satisfaction?

Imagine you are in a clothing store with a child around three years old, and they see something they like. What happens? Most likely, they are screaming "mine!" Imagine a person who likes to treat people, even those not so lovely to them; let's call the people pleasers "givers." There is a correlation between altruism and satisfaction, but satisfaction also correlates with authenticity. Satisfaction is like breathing: You need to inhale and exhale to stay alive. It would be best if you were a giver *and* a taker to become a satisfied person.

Creativity is the level before flow, and it teaches you how to steer your energy. It encourages you to view different angles of your mental health routine. Creativity is the variety you put into sparking your flow state.

Name three activities that spark your creativity:

1. _____

2. _____

3. _____

The activities listed above can also be your hobbies as they are best suited for a flow state. You should lose track of time when doing your hobbies.

The act of flow is a privileged state because of the autonomy to pursue. Due to factors like intergenerational trauma and intersectionality, individuals who would love to enter flow have more obstacles from forces other than their own. Our basic foundation as a child is to be loved, seen, and safe. Many of us have to unlearn the harmful and validated conditions our caregivers have put on us, whether they consciously or subconsciously sabotage a good foundation from childhood.

Intergenerational trauma is a harmful subconscious crack in the foundation passed on from generation to generation. For example, If you have ovaries and your grandma experienced trauma while pregnant with your mother, you inherited that trauma because your mother was born with all her eggs ready, including the egg that created you.

Intersectionality is layers of discrimination that are out of your control. For example, A woman is more oppressed than a man, yet a black woman is more oppressed than a white woman, yet a black trans woman is more oppressed than a black cishet woman. Discrimination and oppression have layers, just like a privilege. For example, the ability to read this book in English is a privilege. Therefore, you are less oppressed and discriminated against than people who can not read English, as they do not receive this information. There is a restriction on people who lack the privileges needed. Some privileges can be learned, like reading English, but others, like white privilege, can not be known.

Scarcity thinking is something folks with intergenerational trauma and intersectionality do because of the lack of resources and the natural loss of dopamine. Scarcity thinking may lead to other negative mindsets like learned helplessness. Learned helplessness is a response to a continuous lack of support towards a goal that ends negatively due to inaction of the participant as it is too mentally painful or exhausting.

The mindset of constantly feeling like you are lacking something in life. The majority of your mental energy goes to negative thoughts surrounding why a situation is or isn't happening to you at the pace you would like it to happen. Scarcity thinking is typically reserved for the lack of money and time, but it can also be a reaction to a history of domestic violence or forms of discrimination. Victimhood is a form of scarcity thinking as the loss of control establishes a connection to a world against the victim. Learned helplessness can also occur alongside scarcity thinking to further push the narrative of an unjust world.

Resilience or Victimhood?

The question now is, are you a victim of your negative thoughts? How much of your daily mental energy do you waste on made-up negative futures? What if I told you there was a way to stop all that mental noise and free up some mental energy? This book will educate you on switching your negative self-talk to positive self-talk by introducing you to the art of abundance thinking. Abundance thinking is the mindset of constantly feeling like there is enough for everyone; very little or if any mental energy goes to either imagining the future or reliving the past. An abundant thinker spends most of their time in the state of now, the present moment.

Learned helplessness is the act of giving up because nothing will change. For example, if you are trying to lose weight and haven't seen any progress for years, you might give up on losing weight. With scarcity thinking, you cannot become motivated and therefore lack all of the levels afterward. It's a sad reality that many individuals face daily and a great example of why everyone needs a support system to hold them accountable to be on track to abundant thinking.

The act of anti-fragility is excellent for combating learned helplessness. Anti-fragility is a framework that works in post-traumatic growth, a realm that prioritizes resistance. Just like how workouts make your body stronger with strength, post-traumatic growth works out your positive mindset after post-traumatic stress.

The "SPIRE" model is an acronym for post-traumatic growth as an indirect way to happiness through overall well-being.

1. **S**piritual
2. **P**hysical
3. **I**ntellectual
4. **R**elational
5. **E**motional

The resilience of anti-fragility comes from the access to happiness being indirect; it must be built into memory by accountability. Accountability can come in many forms, including yourself or your support system.

Spirituality is that sense of purpose you have in your life. You know what you want to do by knowing the answer to the question: *Who am I?*

Without a capitalistic lens, with no talk of wealth or money, answer this question. Remove anything related to your line of work or career if you are not receiving joy from it. Remove any social gender norms as well. What would you be doing if money and society weren't involved? For example, you are a doctor, and your life purpose might be to help people in medical need. Also, remember your life purpose can change throughout your life, and you can have more than one.

Physical is the pressure put on your physical body throughout your life. Not only does it include the amount of stress on your body, but is also related to your lack of recovery.

Questions to ask yourself:

- Can you maintain high energy from day to night?
- Do you have a healthy gut-brain connection?
- Are you sleeping seven to nine hours a night?
- Are you eating healthy throughout the entire day?
- What is your daily amount of exercise?
- Do you experience chronic or acute pain?
- How many times have you experienced burnout?

All these questions are also reflections of self-love: the care and appreciation you give to yourself.

Intellectual is your curiosity about your evolution and your want to continue learning about life. We have all tried to get better at something, and sometimes it takes multiple attempts for success. Each time you try and fail, that is also evolution in motion. The ability to continue asking "why" is vital to a healthy mindset because it is the ability to see innovation. Problems in daily life can never be a one-sided reflection of a story, and a good story has multiple angles to the plot.

Relational has to do with your relationships, your unconditional love support system, and your social life. Due to the global pandemic, social anxiety has gone up because of our lack of human connection for years. But we are lucky to live in an age where the internet exists and virtual social links are still possible.

Emotional is how you appreciate your life through gratitude. Being thankful for what you have received daily is a great way to remove negativity and nervousness quickly.

There will be much relearning regarding social interactions in the coming years.

The level after achieving flow is mastery. Mastery takes at least 10,000 hours to attain the title of expert.

Think of it as *future-proofing*. What is future-proofing? It is the ability to resist change or adapt to change from future situations. For example, if your smartphone gets water damaged, and you have been without a smartphone for some time, your smartphone is your access point to your high-energy playlist. You use your high-energy playlist while you are on your nature walk daily. You could adapt by going on silent nature walks instead of listening to your high-energy playlist and rather listening to the playlist on your laptop afterward. It is not ideal, but you are still achieving the switch from low-energy to high-energy but not with the same speed.

A car can be described as a transport vehicle to one individual, but to another, it could be a place of privacy, and to another, it could be a home. Perspective is everything.

You are the protagonist in the story of your life. How do you understand how the world works from your "main character's" viewpoint?

Let's break it down even more with learning disabilities. Imagine you are an author. You earn your sole income from your mastery of communication on an interest. You also happen to have dyslexia. You are lucky to have a program like a spell check on your phone and laptop. You are in a flow state of creative writing, and a common word that you have spelled by memory escapes you. You repeat the word verbally to try to recall this word. You then try to explain to yourself how it is defined, when you give up trying, you choose to write out the definition in brackets in place of the word, but you now have lost your flow state.

With this example, have you noticed how far away you are from the flow state you were experiencing before this word interrupted and then distracted you? Your mindset will either say that's not fair or how do we fix this?

It takes you at least 15 minutes to get back on track if you have discovered mastery in the art of flow.

So What Do You Do When Your Mind Isn't in a Safer Space?

1. Hold no judgment and focus on *equanimity* (see below). There will be thoughts like "Oh man, I hate when that happens," but one needs to allow these thoughts to enter. Say to the idea, "Thank you for your concern," and show it the exit. Do this for at least five minutes. Start your healing playlist and meditate.
2. Eat if you're hungry and do an activity unrelated to why you need to enter a flow state to remove the pressure for at least 10 minutes, but this could last hours or days. The stress of being away from the flow state needs to be lifted. You need to start over the flow state, not return to the flow state. Increase your frequency with this unrelated activity to give enough distance to increase your energy towards the task that needs the flow state.
3. Welcome back to your flow state.

Equanimity is an even-minded approach to daily obstacles and restrictions in life. You don't have a desire to change the outcome, nor do you have the ability to become dissolved into an obsession. The equanimity state of mind frees you from catastrophic thinking. The main goal of equanimity is to drop the inner resistance as a reaction to your mind's thoughts. Your practice of disconnecting the thoughts with awareness without judgment on how or why the thoughts are there in the first place. This inner resistance can be conscious or even subconscious, and journaling could help release additional tension. Flow is living in the present! Living in the present is a great way to remove the fear of the past or future. Living in the now is the ability to celebrate the little wins. For example, it could be remembering to eat before mental exhaustion. On those sad days, you allow yourself to let go and feel your raw emotions. It is escaping from societal assimilation for that one minute of meditation. Truly living removes all those fake futures and false memories you hoarded in your mindset. This ability to focus on right now, the present moment, is the ultimate goal for meditation. Meditation is just a moment to recover from the daily communications of everyday life. Meditation doesn't look exactly the same for everyone; singing, dancing, and creating are all forms of meditation.

Your Mind and No-Mind

Three things to remember when creating a positive mindset:

1. You are not your mind.
2. The present moment is the only truth.
3. Accept the current time.

The brain is a conditioned tool, and you are not your brain; you are the one with the actual authority. You are just oblivious to being stuck on auto-pilot with your conditioning. The thoughts you are experiencing are conditioned responses to problems from others or observations rather than organic thoughts.

Once you are aware of this self-inquiry, awareness, and mindfulness, you will notice something called "no-mind."

"No-mind" is the gap between the thoughts of fake futures and false memories, the moments of awareness. A simple way to welcome the practice of "no-mind" is becoming hyper-focused on precisely what you are doing in the present moment. For example, imagine you are painting on a canvas on a warm summer day. You are outside, the sun is shining, and you listen to the birds sing. You are painting a landscape of colorful flowers, each different from the next. You make strokes with a brush but also use your fingers. You are enjoying yourself so much that three hours have passed. Then you roll out your yoga mat and start to meditate after such a beautiful flow session. You become an observer without judgment of all the thoughts coming through your mind. You have done this a couple of times and now realize you are now the thinker. You are conscious and subconscious, not the mind. You have noticed that your cravings have disappeared as you realize nothing can make you happy, because happiness is present.

The mind has no power in the present. The reason is that it will always push your thoughts to the past or the future. Your authentic self lives in the now. Time and the mind combine like peanut butter and jelly with a hungry person, and the combination works well to satisfy the hunger. Practice silently watching this interaction of the mind and time.

The Mind in Time

Rejection and guilt live in the past, while desire and consequences are in the future.

Rejection sensitivity (RS) has become more widespread with the global pandemic. Rejection sensitivity is the act of fearing rejection to anxiety; it can make you believe that people will reject you. People with RS have a reaction to this assumption by pushing others away. RS can cause extreme anxiety that affects your daily life by having to avoid specific opportunities or developing social anxiety. Sensitivity to rejection usually has two causes: childhood trauma with neglect and/or ADHD (this condition focuses on creating fake futures and remembering false memories to validate the rejection).

Panic attacks can come from both rejection and guilt. Panic attacks are intense, both physically and mentally. They usually came out of nowhere and typically lasted a short period. One way to calm yourself or others during a panic attack is to start naming colors around you. For example, if you are walking down the street and have a panic attack, you can begin naming anything around you, from the blue car to the green grass to the magenta shoes to the red stop sign. This act will push you into a "no-mind" space and release the mind's grip on you. Remember to breathe in and out slowly while naming the objects and colors.

The future can also cause attacks called anxiety attacks. Anxiety attacks are gradual and can last months. The future thinking of the mind is filled with desires and wants and fearing consequences. Have you ever thought, "why don't I have everything I want yet at my age?" Society also uses the words 'need' and 'want' unchangeably even though they are entirely different words. The need is essential, and a want is a desire, from anxiety about the future to your lack of ability to be grateful for your current blessings in life. Your ability to surrender to the present moment allows you in the flow of universal energy and acceptance of the right now.

Debt and financial stress on the brain will cause anxiety and depression, and blind faith will make it worse. Blind faith is the belief in something without fact-checking. For example, you are spreading fake news without checking references on the information. The only way out of debt and financial stress is to control what you can do, not stress over things you can't control. Focus on your spending of money with a budget, or try something like cash-only spending that may decrease some of your stress.

What is your intention in this life? Isn't it odd how that simple question has so much resistance from the brain?

You are *the* priority in your life. Having less stress in your life is a success. It's the ability to do whatever you need without any added stress. How many of us trade our time for essentials? Yet, this obvious answer is not the social viewpoint on life. The community wants you to become a good citizen as well. Those shared morals allow you to access altruism, and through activism, you are met with that unwelcome question—take a moment and ponder once more...

What Is Your Intention in This Life?

Brainstorm possible reasons for your conscious intention to continue to live without judgment.

List at least five reasons for the intention to continue.

1. _____

2. _____

3. _____

4. _____

5. _____

Are there any connections to the reasons listed above?

For example, if you listed all names of your family members, your conscious intention for the subconscious agreement to continue existence is your family, and your legacy will continue that intention past the physical form. Legacy is how you are remembered after you are gone from the physical form by living people. Generational wealth is the ability to have continuous wealth to fund your legacy in global culture.

How do you personally define the term culture? You might also have more than one culture. You most likely have more than one culture, for example, a home, work, city, country, and tribe culture, to name a few.

Use this as an example:

- *Home culture*: South Asian and Caribbean
- *Work culture*: Remote and Entrepreneurial
- *City culture*: Toronto
- *Country*: Canada
- *Tribe culture*: Artistic Unity

Your turn! List at least five of your cultures below:

- *Home culture:* _____
- *Work culture:* _____
- *City culture*: _____
- *Country*: _____
- *Tribe culture*: _____

Tribe culture is the description of your ideal support system for maximum evolution. Chosen members of your support system are the cheerleaders for your life's purpose.

Are you part of a positively or negatively viewed culture in society? Certain cultures are seen negatively globally: such as the black experience of dehumanization, and yet the perspective of white supremacy is seen as positive to some due to their pride in colonialism. This positive globalization of whiteness is why people who identify as white can not experience racism but can experience discrimination due to their race. The bias of the white race does not negate the positive global view of whiteness as "civilized."

Socioeconomic status (SES) matters, and the most marginalized people on the planet have a lot of intersectionalities and trauma. SES is the economic and social privilege you have in society.

If you are from a globally viewed culture, remove all the negative aspects as they are most likely put there by intersectionality and intergenerational trauma.

Is the definition of culture intrinsically motivated or extrinsic motivated, to you?

For example, if global media negatively view your culture, that is most likely a perspective of someone who is not part of the culture and, therefore, does not have a proper perspective of your culture; it's an outside observation.

We are all beautiful humans, and we make mistakes, and as a global culture, we need to be humble in that aspect. But with our known intersectionalities. For example, two individuals are women and are both members of the Asian community. Both individuals can be discriminated against or taken advantage of based on those intersectionalities, but one individual is a single mum, and her intersectionality of being a mother has more layers to her discrimination or can affect her SES in her life.

A great example of this intersectionality of culture in a song is Kendrick Lamar's "The Heart Part 5." The music video shows examples of black men who have intersectionality to their experience in society. As they are all part of the black experience, it's irrelevant if they have made mistakes, they are still part of the unique experience of being a black man in society. There is so much more in the music video as "The Heart" series he puts out are reflections on how he is feeling in the world in the spring of 2022.

Here are some more questions to further understand your unique culture(s):

- What are the stereotypes associated with your culture(s)?

- How is intersectionality managed in your culture(s)?
- How is mental health managed in your culture(s)?
- How are stress and rest viewed in your culture(s)?

You need to actively practice altruism and accept your authenticity to feel daily satisfaction. Being multicultural is complex and might be part of your intersectionality, and this might have its unique situations to sort out. Talk therapy has been very successful at navigating this complexity.

Set up a daily routine to continue good energy to attract a flow state.

The element of flow starts with curiosity, and that curiosity needs to be a daily priority to excel to mastery level. Mastery is the result of the development of flow. You will quickly get to access flow by practicing your daily routine at this state.

Keep in mind that engagement of the flow state is a privilege. Some individuals will never be able to access this privilege because of the inability to remove themselves from a survival state of mind. To access the flow state, you need to access a safer space and have the ability to thrive in life. Your essentials for survival need to be met like shelter, food, water, and unconditional love.

Future-proofing is a must; your brain is a tool like an algorithm and will continuously push you into the past or future. The push comes from extrinsic motivation programming and is not programmed by your inner motivation. The goal is to focus on the present. With the power of now, you will access the power of stability of the mind. Equanimity is the ability to be indifferent to any situation and not take it personally.

Checklist

- Continue your daily gratitude journal and write at least one sentence per day.
- On a separate page, write your music journal entry after listening to the song: "Look at This (Remix)" by Tribe Called Red. How did the music make you feel?
- Journal prompt: Have you ever experienced flow?
- Make a daily routine for yourself with at least five steps.
- Continue your meditation.
- Continue your minimalistic cleanse.

Chapter 5

Letting Go

Beat It, Negative Energy!

Binaural beats are a quick way to change your energy from low to high in a short time. Sound therapy works with frequencies to alter your vibrations. These vibrations are what change your energy levels. Each binaural beat has a different reason for its frequency change.

Are you working at a high or low frequency when doing a project? Binaural beats in beta frequency can help you reach high frequency to maintain flow for a particular project if needed. Isochronic tones are not continuous like binaural beats, which comes down to preference.

What are binaural beats and how can they help with flow?

A *binaural beat* is a difference between many two different frequencies heard simultaneously. For example, a 100hz in the left earplug and a 130hz in the right earplug; therefore, the binaural beat is 30hz, which would make it a gamma frequency in binaural beats.

There are five types of binaural beats:

- Gamma frequency is at a difference of 30–50 Hz.
- Beta frequency is at a difference of 13–3 Hz.
- Alpha frequency is at a difference of 7–13 Hz.
- Theta frequency is at a difference of 4–7 Hz.
- Delta frequency is at a difference of 0.5–4 Hz.

Binaural beats are a quick way to change your frequency from low to high in a short time.

Each binaural beat has a different reason for its frequency change:

- Gamma will wake you up.
- Beta will keep you focused.
- Alpha will help you reflect on life.
- Delta will put you to sleep.
- Theta will remove anxiety.

You can find these binaural beats on youtube. The best way to listen to them is without ads and in their pure form without music added.

A way to experience this in nature is listening to frogs crip; they crip at a frequency of 180 Hz, which will promote relaxation and reduce anxiety. This natural frequency can mimic the benefits of binaural beats by communicating between two frogs with their slight frequency difference, just like having slightly different frequencies in each earplug.

Another way to increase energy is through evolution, exploring discourse and tensions in your community through reaction. A change in perspective can lead to a high frequency. For example, stand-up comedy is where comedians express their observations on the world. A great punchline is unannounced and unexpected. To effectively change your energy level from low to high, you must genuinely enjoy the comedian's set.

Change is the natural way of progress in life and is the only consistency we have.

Letting go is the release of excess control and responsibility for yourself:

- "no-doing"
- embracing change
- not focusing on outcomes
- letting go of excess

The act of "no-doing" is like farming. The crop will need initial help with planting, watering, and access to the sun. After the initial extrinsic motivation by you, you must let the crop start its intrinsic motivation. This allowance of the self-motivation of others is the act of letting go of control.

Embracing change will give you so much energy, as resisting change is an extreme energy waster. Adjusting this mindset into embracing change will give you all that wasted energy back, and you can now prioritize it for something else. You are the authority figure in your life.

Not focusing on outcomes will remove the pressure you place on yourself and allow you to focus on the flow mindset flourishing.

Letting go of excess is just that. Removing all non-essentials.

Temporary Pleasure Exercises

These are activities for you to practice the art of letting go. The activities must have a brief lifespan; no permanent element at all.

Some examples are:

- You can blow bubbles and enjoy the colors in the bubbles. This activity can range in the size of bubbles, and you can add even the sense of smell.
- You can draw abstract chalk graffiti with no direction, then allow your imagination to connect the dots and create an artistic masterpiece. You can enjoy adding to your creation until it rains or washes it off. This activity can range in the size of the wall involved, and you can use an array of different colored chalk.
- Cloud gazing is the act of witnessing cloud formation and using your imagination to create a temporary window into personal perspective as no one will see the same cloud imagination image.

Permanent and Long-Term Exercises

Journaling is a great way to empty negative thoughts when overthinking—similar to taking out the trash to make room for more junk. Why not learn to produce less waste and have a smaller carbon footprint by practicing minimalism with waste consumption? The same goes for negative thoughts and overthinking; overthinking leads to an overwhelming feeling of anxious energy, which is a low frequency. Writing is an effective way to combat overthinking. The more you write, the less overthinking you will do. A daily journal comes in to combat daily negative thoughts of overthinking. Your daily journal can consist of anything you can do with a writing tool like a pen or pencil and a notebook. We will concentrate on daily journaling as a form of creative writing.

Start with the date and a journal entry with a minimum of one sentence and no maximum length. You can buy a pre-made journal or make one yourself, but give yourself at least 180 pages. Find out if you prefer a pen or pencil as your writing tool and begin. You don't have to write in your journal every day, but the ideal end goal is to document your emotions, experiences, and observations on a daily occurrence. Your emotions are in control when you are journaling. It is like you are trauma dumping or love bombing, but without a victim—trauma dumping is the act of offloading your trauma to someone without permission or triggering them; love bombing gives an overwhelming and uncomfortable amount of affection to an individual in manipulation and is abusive behavior. These acts can leave people with auto-immune diseases or mental health problems drained for days or weeks. A daily journal is safer for intensive personal emotions like trauma or affection. A safer space is a supportive place where you feel comfortable sharing your vulnerability without judgment or fear of discrimination. When journaling, it is essential to be in a physically safer space where you are neither disrupted nor interrupted, as this will disconnect your journal entry. A great way to start journaling is to do the one-minute journal exercise, writing as much or as little as you want in one minute. Journal prompts are also a fitting place to start, and these prompts are questions or phases to help inspire you to write your journal entry.

There are no rules to the writing in the journal, as this form of creative writing is full of emotions, and grammar and punctuation are entirely at the mercy of the emotions. Some people even write their journals in code to keep the contents secret. Journaling is usually written in the first person. This style of creative writing can beautifully show the development of a person in a very vulnerable and intimate way. A journal is a recording of how you feel that day at that exact moment. For example, your goal is that you want to change to a neutral reaction to triggers you encounter; with a daily journal, you can watch the goal progress, succeed, or fail, and with that curial information, you can either continue with success or make the necessary changes to attempt success again! Daily journaling makes sure you have documentation with all those goal recipients. So you can make an educated decision instead of continuing the attempt to be content with failure for now. Ultimately the choice is yours. A daily journal is an excellent tool if you want to change your life.

Daily journaling is excellent for your mental health, especially for depression and anxiety.

What's the difference between a journal and a diary? It's like scrapbooking compared to all the photos stored on your smartphone. Scrapbooking is a diary, and your photo history is a journal. A daily journal is a daily log of your emotions, experiences, and observations, while a diary is a unique log of memorable moments in your life. It's also completely okay to have both as they are entirely different creative writing styles.

The safer space will allow for communication with your inner child. This conscious and subconscious connection This conscious and subconscious connection is vital for the success of subconscious manifestation.

Future writing is a creative exercise that allows you to write about the future in the present tense. Create a hypothetical positive story about obstacles or restrictions stopping your evolution and include triumphs and celebrations you want to have in your future, in the present tense as if you already have it.

Practice *living democracy*: Use a talking circle to reawaken empathy within your support system. Have everyone sit in a circle and discuss the support team's current thoughts. Ensure there is some indicator of who's turn; it is like a talking piece to ensure respect of speech. People in the circle can talk about anything on their minds, from negative or positive experiences they are currently dealing with or experiences that have lingered.

There might be a time in the future when your doctor will prescribe experience over medication. When you enter a flow state, you have successfully switched to your peak performance frequency, a place higher than high frequency. You will remember very well as hyper-focused, and time will pass very strangely. When you are suffering from heartbreak, grief, or addiction, the flow state is strong enough to overload the memories in question and lessen the power of the reminder over your mindset.

The American army had a study where soldiers diagnosed with post-traumatic stress disorder (PTSD) participated in talk therapy and the activity of surfing. Five weeks after the experiment, the soldiers had an extreme drop in their symptoms or had been cured of PTSD.

Post-traumatic growth (PTG) is the psychological change in your mindset from intrinsic motivation. PTG is a change in your perspective on understanding how the world operates and, therefore, a shift in perspective on your perceived trauma's power over your mindset. You shift from the trauma state of survival to the PTG state of thriving in life.

Binaural beats and a playlist of songs you connect with are excellent forms of sound therapy to achieve PTG. Sound therapy is the act of healing through sound, and throughout this book, you have been receiving healing songs to form a mini healing playlist to start your journey with sound therapy.

This evolution with perspective change will allow the mind to start becoming curious and start engaging with the importance of letting go and productivity. Letting go is the link to the push of accessing your positive mindset to change your perspective on your problems, and that's because the flow state is fantastic. It is the feeling of being "high on life" without the use of drugs.

The act of letting go of excess through minimalism is something you have been practicing throughout this book. If you are experiencing difficulties letting go of excess, try to focus on temporary beauty and allow yourself to do exercises like blowing bubbles, chalk drawing, or cloud gazing.

Taking up journaling is an easy and cost-effective way to dump your problems onto paper and let them go instead of trauma bonding (over-attachment to an abuser or to the cycle of abuse). If a physical journal is out of your budget, try a digital journal as it is very eco-friendly.

Talking circles, or spaces where equal sharing is encouraged and cultivated, are essential to the social human experience. The best way to succeed in life is through mentorship and learning how others have gained their success. Talking circles are a form of support group, and the individual involved can tell you what to avoid and steer you in the right direction to your goals.

Experience is a great healer, while people might also need medication. But many times, medication and drugs are the first response and can be a distraction from the causes of mental health issues. It is scary, but facing your anxieties and depression in life can be resolved by removing the validation of fake futures and false memories to reset the mindset to a positive state.

Checklist

- Listen to a binaural beat frequency of your choice, and write a journal entry on how the binaural beat frequency made you feel.
- Attend a talking circle.
- Do a temporary pleasure exercise.
- Continue your meditation.
- Continue your minimalistic cleanse.

Conclusion

The word "allow" has been used in this book a lot, and it's on purpose. It is to stress that you are the authority figure in your life. We have been taught repeatedly that our input doesn't matter in society—but that is learned helplessness. The truth is that your opinion matters! Your negative opinion of yourself significantly influences your mindset. Change your negative view of yourself into a positive one and step back to watch the spontaneous improvement in your overall mental health.

You Are the Authority Figure in Your Life, Not Your Mind

Witness this awareness with meditation and become the observer of these external thoughts. Let them get your attention, listen to their concerns, and politely ask them to leave your mind. This practice will take some patience but trust in the process, and you will one day be free of the negative put-downs others have planted in your subconscious. Allow awe to take you over your brain and remind you how small your problems are compared to the universe.

Use a whiteboard to write down two columns:

- **Urgent:** For things that need to be done today, with a maximum of five to seven items.
- **Important:** For essential things for the current week, with a maximum of five to seven items.

Flow is essential for increased productivity of your spiritual growth, as said previously, but your reaction to a problem is what your brain, as a tool, documents. Through the self-exploration you have done through this book, act from a place of listening and understanding rather than a place of reaction and response; hopefully you can hold a safer space for all humanity in your heart. The altruism you give to others and acceptance of authenticity will guide you to the peace you desperately crave: the satisfaction of life—a life where you are happy and content with what will be, all that is, and all that ever will be, through equanimity.

Your Healing Playlist

1. "Good Job" by Alicia Keys
2. "Relax, Take It Easy" by Mika
3. "Acouscous" by Emawk
4. "Look at This (Remix)" by Tribe Called Red
5. the binaural beat frequency of your choice

The first three songs on the healing playlist are all about validating your progress on this journey, celebrating taking the risk to better yourself, and giving yourself the ability to rest. The fourth song is about activating, connecting you to a higher frequency, and is done with fewer vocals and a faster tempo. The indigenous origins will allow you to connect easily with nature. Lastly, depending on the binaural beat you choose, you could experience insight into your conscious and subconscious, concentration of focus on a goal, relaxation, and reflection on how you let yourself recover, extended flow states, and deep healing through sleep.

What else is on your playlist?

Thank you so much for reading this book. I hope you are inspired and motivated to chase your dream of a positive mindset with your daily problems. Remember, patience is critical for this journey! Please go easy on yourself and come from a place of non-judgment and unconditional love for yourself.

You deserve an inner monologue that is on your side.

Peace & Love.

References

Breland-Noble, A. M. (2020). *Community mental health engagement with racially diverse populations.* Academic Press.

Carmichael, E. (2022, May 2). *How to become more effective and productive in everything you do!* | Jay Shetty | Top 10 Rules. Www.youtube.com. https://www.youtube.com/watch?v=DLgMjNda9Mg

Chaieb, L., Wilpert, E. C., Reber, T. P., & Fell, J. (2015). Auditory beat stimulation and its effects on cognition and mood states. *Frontiers in Psychiatry*, 6(70). https://doi.org/10.3389/fpsyt.2015.00070

Chapman, G. D., & Summers, A. (2010). *The five love languages: How to express heartfelt commitment to your mate.* Lifeway Press.

Deci, E. L., & Ryan, R. M. (1985). *Intrinsic motivation and self-determination in human behavior.* Springer Science & Business Media.

Garcia-Argibay, M., Santed, M. A., & Reales, J. M. (2018). Efficacy of binaural auditory beats in cognition, anxiety, and pain perception: A meta-analysis. *Psychological Research*, 83(2), 357–372. https://doi.org/10.1007/s00426-018-1066-8

Godin, S., & Macleod, H. (2012). *V is for vulnerable: Life outside the comfort zone.* Portfolio/Penguin.

Harvey, S. (2018). *Jump: Take the leap of faith to achieve your life of abundance* (p. 196). Amistad Press. (Original work published 2017)

Infurna, F. J., & Luthar, S. S. (2016). Resilience to major life stressors is not as common as thought. *Perspectives on Psychological Science*, 11(2), 175–194. https://doi.org/10.1177/1745691615621271

Is A Joke, N. (2022, May 5). *Snoop Dogg: Full interview with Arsenio Hall | Netflix is a joke: The festival.* Www.youtube.com. https://www.youtube.com/watch?v=xGx1nUrkCSg

Jorgenson, E. (2020). *The almanack of Naval Ravikant: A guide to wealth and happiness.* Magrathea Publishing.

Joshua Fields Millburn, & Nicodemus, R. (2017). *Minimalism.* Sydney, New Hachette Australia.

Kotler, S., & Wheal, J. (2017). *Stealing fire how silicon valley, the navy seals, and maverick scientists are revolutionizing the way we live and work.* Dey Street Books.

Loftus, E. (2013, June). *Transcript of "How reliable is your memory?"* Www.ted.com. https://www.ted.com/talks/elizabeth_loftus_how_reliable_is_your_memory/transcript?language=en

McIntosh, J. (2018, July 16). *15 benefits of drinking water and other water facts.* Www.medicalnewstoday.com. https://www.medicalnewstoday.com/articles/290814

Moore, L. (2018). *How to be alone: If you want to, and even if you don't.* Atria Paperback.

Morin, A. (2021, August 23). *Why some people more sensitive to rejection than others.* Verywell Mind. https://www.verywellmind.com/what-is-rejection-sensitivity-4682652#:~:text=Individuals%20who%20are%20high%20in

Norman Vincent Peale. (2005). *The power of positive thinking; and, the amazing results of positive thinking.* Fireside/Simon & Schuster.

Oppland, M. (2019, July 16). *8 ways to create flow according to Mihaly Csikszentmihalyi [+TED talk].* PositivePsychology.com. https://positivepsychology.com/mihaly-csikszentmihalyi-father-of-flow/

Padmanabhan, R., Hildreth, A. J., & Laws, D. (2005). A prospective, randomised, controlled study examining binaural beat audio and pre-operative anxiety in patients undergoing general anaesthesia for day case surgery.

Anaesthesia, 60(9), 874–877. https://doi.org/10.1111/j.1365-2044.2005.04287.x

Parris, K. M., Velik-Lord, M., & North, J. M. A. (2009). Frogs call at a higher pitch in traffic noise. *Ecology and Society,* 14(1). https://doi.org/10.5751/es-02687-140125

Ryan, R. M., & Deci, E. L. (2000). *Intrinsic and extrinsic motivations: Classic definitions and new directions* (pp. 54–67). S.N.

Schwartz, D. J. (2015). *The magic of thinking big.* Touchstone.

Shetty, J. (2020). *Think like a monk: Train your mind for peace and purpose every day.* Simon & Schuster.

Tal Ben-Shahar. (2021). *Happier, no matter what: Finding pleasure and purpose in hard times.* Experiment Llc.

Talk, R. T. (2022, May 6). *Red table talk: Dr. Alfiee | Types of depression | Facebook.* Www.facebook.com. https://www.facebook.com/watch/?v=678466576591793

talks, T. (2017). *All the lonely people | Karen Dolva | TEDxArendal* [YouTube Video]. YouTube. https://www.youtube.com/watch?v=j-Gil9l8yIE

talks, T. (2020, July 9). *Being alone isn't being lonely | Ankit Shah | TEDxPineCrestSchool.* Www.youtube.com. https://www.youtube.com/watch?v=4W1E6m1EUAU

Tolle, E. (2004). *The power of NOW: A guide to spiritual enlightenment.* Namaste Pub.; Novato, Calif.

Vincenty, S. (2021, June 23). *The signs of a trauma bonded relationship can sneak up on you.* Oprah Daily. https://www.oprahdaily.com/life/relationships-love/a36788688/what-is-trauma-bonding/

Yusim, A., & Grigaitis, J. (2020). Efficacy of binaural beat meditation technology for treating anxiety symptoms: A pilot study. *The Journal of Nervous and Mental Disease,* 208(2), 155–160. https://doi.org/10.1097/NMD.0000000000001070

Printed in Great Britain
by Amazon

83527882R00058